# WORDSMITH'S WANDERINGS

TED MORGAN

First published in Hardback 2014 by Violet Circle Publishing

ISBN 978-1-910299-04-3

Cover illustration and all Photographs by Edward Morgan

British Library Cataloguing in Publication Data.

A catalogue record for this book is available from the British
Library.

www.violetcirclepublishing.co.uk

info@violetcirclepublishing.co.uk

Dedicated to the memory of

My darling wife

Pat


1944-2013

I have been writing verse for many years mainly for my own amusement.

Now at 76 I have recently had the courage to allow other people to see my efforts. My poems and verse cover a wide range of situations both humorous and sad.

I have been encouraged to produce this small volume by my son, and also  by other friends and family who have been reading my poetry on my blog, I do hope that you enjoy my efforts.

# THE WORDSMITH

I think I'll write a poem; a wordsmith I will be,
But what the heck to write about has put me all at sea,
So I thought that I would Google, the different types of verse,
I think that was a bad idea, it made my thought block worse,
I found that verse was graded into many different kinds,
It seemed it was dependent on the rhyming of the lines
In descriptive poems you visualise the objects of your verse,
But writing in reflective mode your thoughts are more
diverse,
The poem in the narrative vein has a story it must tell,
Whilst odes entwine a person or an object in its spell,
The ballad it is musical and has a certain rhythm,
The lyric like the ballad is tuneful, short in vision.
Now Shakespeare he wrote sonnets in a very special way
Whilst melancholic elegies where the forte of Mr. Grey,
And last of all the limerick made up of lines times five,
And naughty verse has sometimes made this latter one
survive,
With all these different kinds of verse my brain cells start to
twirl,
I don't know which one I will choose, to write my poetic
pearl,
After hours of fruitless thinking I have a writer's block
My brain cells decommissioned like a ship that's in dry dock!

This is one of my first poems, written in 1968 when I was in hospital for three months.

# <u>FLOWERS</u>

Flowers can say in so many ways,

Emotions that we all portray,

In sorrow or in gladness too,

They can express so much to you.


Roses, Tulips and Daffodils,

Are given with grace in joy or ill,

A wreath, a cross a posy small,

Say so much when all words fail.


We in our lives do emulate the flower,

In all its stages from bud to death,

We should not ever fail to find expression,

For what we feel is mirrored in a flower.

# "MUCKY PUP"

When I was young my mum was there, to wipe a tear or straighten hair,

Oh! I was such a mucky pup, who never did like washing up,

But walked around with wrinkled socks, dirty shoes and mud stained tops,

And played in all the grubby places, amidst my friends with dirt stained faces.

On getting home from school each day, the cry was

"mum can I go out and play?"

I see that look upon her face, he'll come back looking a disgrace,

But never mind I know that he, will always be back home for tea:

She was to me the ideal mum, but she did occasionally smack my "bum".

When I transgressed my mum's rules, and was reported for cheek at school.

"Respect your elders" mum would say, and never lie or truant play

Learn all you can when you're school, and never ever play the fool,

4

You want a good report this term, a "good job" will be your return.

I remember now those golden days, when all I had to do was play,

And watch my mum do all the chores, at "dolly tub" and washing board,

Oh! How I wish that she could see, the mucky child that used to be,

For now I am at sixty four, cleaner than in days of yore.

But still if unobserved, can be, that mucky child from '43

# THE PEG RUG

We wanted a rug for the kitchen, Mum was fed up with Lino on't floor,

But we had no money to buy one; and hard Lino was making her feet sore,

The only thing for it was to make one, not like Wilton or things that were posh,

But a rug made with bits of a blanket or a coat that had just had a wash,

Mum never liked throwing away clothing, make do and mend was the aim

For in wartime you had to be careful, that was all part of the game

I watched as she started to cut coat up, in strips about three inches long,

Then got an old peg that was broken, and a sack for the backing that's strong,

She pushed bits of cloth through the canvas, each strip very close to the next,

And slowly she worked her way forward, in a pattern that seemed quite complex,

In the evenings when house work were over, she sat with peg rug on her knee,

It grew as the evenings passed by like, mum fortified by big cups of tea,

Came the day when the rug it were finished,

resplendent in red blue and green,

And when put on the floor in the kitchen, it was best rug that I'd ever seen!

I roamed the Derbyshire Peak District both in my youth and also as a Member of a Mountain Rescue Team for many years. I was sitting at my desk one day recently and in my mind's eye came a view of the Dark Peak. This is my poem of praise for that wild and beautiful part of the country.

# THE DARK PEAK

The grit stone stands as a sentinel to the Dark Peak,
And moorland stretches as far as the eye can see,
 Peat bogs lie in wait to catch the unwary traveller,
Grouse disturbed by wandering feet, fly low with raucous cry,
The wind blows over the plateau, you hear its plaintive song,
And clouds drift silently over swaying purple heather,
Stone walls in regimented lines climb to distant hills,
Whilst sheep munch silently on the tufted grass,
This wonderland of nature carved by earthly movement;
With towering cliffs of darkened stone and tumbling
waterfalls,
Still tarns enclosed in silent valleys;
Enhance the rugged beauty of the scene.

## IN MEMORY OF PRIVATE WILLIAM MORGAN

## NO 48836   MANCHESTER REGIMENT

My Dad fought in the First World War and like many others suffered from the effects of that horrific conflict until his untimely death the day after my 9<sup>th</sup> birthday 1n 1947.

## THIS IS DEDICATED TO HIM.

My dad joined the Manchester's, when General Kitchener called,

He donned the khaki uniform and marched off with his pals,

The bands they were a playing, and boots they tramped in time,

And he proudly marched through waving crowds, of people stood in line.

He trained and camped at Heaton Park, on the edge of the town,

They taught him how to shoot and charge, and cut the Hun right down,

And how to dig a deep, deep trench, wood sides and sandbagged lined

To keep them safe from snipers with their rifle sights aligned.

When trained, to France they sent him; and at first it was a breeze,

Not near the line of battle, he was safe and  much at ease;

Midst all the General Officers who planned the Somme offensives,

They planned attacks in safety, far from the front line trenches.

Then he moved up to the front line, amid all the mud and shells,

Midst death and devastation 'twas the anteroom of Hell,

First the barrage; then the whistle sounds; over the top they go,

With bayonets drawn, charging forward, towards the German foe.

Then all went black: next time he was aware,

A German tongue he heard, around his head a bandage,

Shot in the head, and left for dead, but found by German foe,

Who carried him to their aid post, that treated all laid low.

In later years he did not speak of the horrors of the war

The man who came back from the dead,

Was not the same, as the man who went to war,

Images of conflict disturbed his nights of rest,

He died at 55 a sick and troubled man.

But as a dad, he was, to me the best.

# REMEMBRANCE

From cenotaph to village small, a bugle sounds the
plaintive call,
And warriors from a time long past, old comrades they
recall;
Each year they come, though numbers dwindle
But their duty they express
To honour friends now at rest, no longer clad in
battledress,
The last post sounds and tears in many eyes are found,
Remembering friends and comrades, who lie in foreign
ground
We who are left must not forget, the sacrifice they
made.
We benefit today from their sacrificial foundation laid,
So as we gather round memorial plaques, and
monuments of stone
And read the names inscribed, never should we our lot
bemoan,
For men have died, to see our right to freedom won,
We say our thanks with wreaths of poppies on stones
laid.

# NATIONAL SERVICE THE FIRST SIX WEEKS

When I was 18 I had to go in the forces to do National Service. Like many lads of my era it was quite an experience. This poem charts the first few weeks in the forces at a "square bashing" initial training camp. No matter which service you went into the experience was the same. The events in this poem are all based on fact but with a slightly humorous twist!

The government decided, to make of me a man,
And call me up for service in our countries infantry
I just did not reckon on the trauma that ensued
To make soldier out of me just proved that I'd been screwed,
The first thing that they did to me was shave off all my hair.
Then fitted me with a uniform, the fit just caused despair,
The tunic it was rather tight, the trousers long and baggy
The look was more deformed than trim, untidy loose and craggy.
Next thing I knew, they threw at me a lot of soldier junk,
Like button sticks and sewing kits and pimply boots that stunk
A rifle and my webbing was next just hung on me
And off I went to the billet like a festooned Christmas tree.
A "kindly" corporal he took charge and showed me to my bed
He did not kiss me like my mum but kicked my ass instead,
He told me to "get felled in with the other useless tykes",

Then proceeded to berate us and tell us of his likes.

"Get up at six and have a shower and make sure you chin is shaved,"

And always wash both "fore and aft" so the crabs will not invade,

Make sure that kit is always clean and trousers creased and neat like,

Your bed pack done with blankets six, and the bottom sheet pulled tight.

Next on to the parade ground to learn our left from right,

The Corporal he had us marching from dawn until the night,

He shouted "you're a shower" "You're daft and most unsightly",

I did not mind him shouting but please do it more politely!

The Sergeant he was even worse and his language most impressive,

Thought I don't think he went to Oxford he was far too too aggressive,

He thought that when we were born, the wrong part was thrown away,

The fact that we could not march filled him with such dismay

When we went to fire a rifle things got from bad to worse,

The thing just bucked and kicked us, and made the corporal curse

"Hold it tight, look down the sight and pull the trigger slowly,"

Said in such a way that it sounded, "padre like" and holy

We were introduced to an officer when the billet he inspected,

Picked up a carpet at the door and said "this thing's infected,"

The floor it was not clean enough, our boots had not been polished,

And the place it was a shambles so all privileges abolished.

The cookhouse was the center our "gourmet eating place"

Egon Rony dubbed the mess, a "ruddy big disgrace."

They served us bully beef for sure, and kind of rubber eggs

And pint pots of coloured liquid that were made from coffee dregs?

So to the NAFFI we did go to drowned ourselves with drink,

Cups of char and NAFFI wads to put us in the pink,

But sadly they did not work, for as you all can tell,

The next day brought the dawning of another day of hell.

Whilst there, we had a medical it really was a hoot

The M.O looked us over, but he was pickled as a newt,

If you had pulse and stood still you're guaranteed A 1!

And then a large dose of laxative to make sure that you could run

We endured this for six long weeks and started getting better,

And learnt to obey orders, right down to the last letter

They organised a big parade so we could all Pass Out,

And invited friends and family, so there could be no doubt.

The cream of England's men folk were on parade that day,

And complicated marching drill made sure we earned our pay,

Chests out with pride we shouldered arms and marched in time t'band,

National Service soldiers the finest in the land.

I have always loved nature and the changing seasons the following poems are all based around this theme

# SPRING

New life from the ground bursts free from winter frosts,
And crocus peep their heads above the earth to catch the
morning sun,
Birds are busy flying to and fro with twigs to weave into a nest
Trees discard dull winters skeletal shape and burst into bud;
to leave the woodlands ablaze with myriad leaves of different
hues,
Migrant birds arrive from warmer climes and fill the air with
springtime song,
The joy of spring is in new beginnings; bluebells in woodland
glades,
Daffodils and tulips swaying in the March breeze,
Even April showers help to nurture this cavalcade of
new-born life,
Whilst man looks on in awesome wonder at this changing scene.

# SUMMER

The sun high in the sky, nature's colours seem so
bright,

Swallows and swifts and starlings in swooping endless
flight,

The scent of flowers drifting on the whispering gentle
breeze,

And bees surround the blossoms and pollen laden
trees,

A flash of colour on the riverbank as the kingfisher
hunts its prey,

The sights and sounds of summer on a warm idyllic
day,

Hedgerows filled with flowers that peep out from leafy
hides,

Show butterflies with wings bedecked; like smiling
summer brides,

How I wish that it could last, and warmth fill all our
days,

But summer leads to autumn and our harvest songs of
praise.

# THOUGHTS OF AUTUMN

The mornings cool, and leaves are slowly changing,

The autumn creeps its way to muted hues,

Where once green and vibrant woodland stood,

Its leaves are fading to yellow and russet brown,

Waiting for the northern winds to blow and scatter them;

Some birds migrate to warmer climes,

And squirrels look to hide and sleep away the winter chill,

Whilst shorter days give way to sparkling star lit nights,

And howling winds give notice of a winter yet to come.

# WINTER

It gets so cold in winter, for the wind howls through the trees,

And Jack Frost weaves his magic, causing pools and streams to freeze,

Whilst birds all crowd together as protection from the cold,

The bright stars twinkle in the sky, with the moon a disc of gold,

At dawn the world is waking to a pale and dismal day,

And the howling wind amidst the trees causes branch and twig to sway,

A nature-caused fandango with all bush and tree in time,

Whilst Birch and Oak and Rowan keep in time with swaying Lime,

The winter day is far removed from summer's heady heights,

The days are short and soon give way to long and frost filled nights,

And then the snow begins to fall and trees in ermine stoles are crowned,

The hunting owl glides silently across his frosty hunting ground,

So winter slowly spans the days until the snowdrops show,

And underneath the frozen ground the bulbs and corms do grow,

They burst their heads above the ground from their winter time sojourn,

They want to herald springtime when warmth and sun return.

This was written as a song and was often performed when I sang and played in a folk group called the Ringley Folk it was also broadcast on Radio Manchester in a live session from the Horseshoe Pub in Ringley.

# SEASONS

Moorland surrounds most Lancashire towns,
With cotton mills empty of working men's sounds,
Amidst all this desolate neglect and decay,
Wild flowers grow to brighten your day,
Heather it grows for mile upon mile,
Midst those bleak hills of peat and of mire,
Farmers try hard to make ends meet,
With sheep and stone walls round their lonely retreat;
The autumn steals in and all colours fade;
To the rusts and the browns in moorland and glade,
Amidst fading colours and shortening of days,
On purple heather the sunlight still plays;
In winter the wind from the north it doth blow,
Bringing drifts and starvation along with the snow,
The fells they are mantled in a white ermine stole,
Whilst rivers are stilled to a slow icy flow;
In springtime the hills awake from their sleep,
To the sound of the lambs and the sheep's plaintive bleat,
The hills are awakening to the thrill of the call,
Of curlew and plover flying high overall;
The summer is next in this seasonal sweep,
The long days of light allow little sleep,
The fells radiate with warm breezy days,
And the gorse growing wild adds its scent to the haze,
Seasons may come and seasons may go,
And life like a river continues to flow.

# REFLECTIONS ON AUTUMN

We speak of autumn as the season of change,
A myriad shades of colour light up our trees,
The russet browns and vivid red of falling leaves.
The trees slowly shed their leaves to leave a ghostly frame.
The winds start to blow and days get shorter.
The sun sinks low on the horizon; we see the light begin to fade.
Flowers lose their tossing heads; some just die in the cold winds.
The earth prepares to feel the chill of the oncoming winter season.
Whilst we humans speak of the autumn of our years.
The time of quiet reflection, of memories of days long gone.
We feel the pain of friends and relations departing this life.
Some relish the quietude of this period of their lives.
A time to explore new horizons, seek new challenges.
For our long winter will come and we know not when.

# FROSTY MORNING

On a cold frosty morning when the air is still,

The frost it glistens on the window and the sill,

The dawn is just breaking and silence surrounds,

And sparkling like crystal, the hoar-frost abounds,

Jack frosts works his magic whilst most mortals sleep,

Dawn slowly breaks, and the sun starts to peep;

Fills the earth with its glory, as we rise from our beds

Whilst the crocus and snowdrops lift up frosted heads,

Another day dawns with a sky azure blue,

And bird song welcomes a new day for you.

# TREES

You walk into a woodland, midst Oak and Ash and Larch,
And enter into a magic world where branches twist and arch,
But woods are special places for birds and plants and deer,
The dwelling place of mighty Hearn that evil spirits fear.

The mighty Oak it stands supreme, its trunk all gnarled with age,
Whilst its canopy spreads far and wide as its acorns are displayed,
It gave us wood to build great ships and a navy of renown,
And ships that traded far and wide gaining countries for our crown.

The Ash was once a sacred tree, of the Nordic tribes,
And Odin carved a man of Ash, it's said it came alive,
Its wood was used for furniture and tools and also skis,
Some forms do weep and you will hear them rustle in the breeze,

The Mountain Ash or Rowan kept the witchs from your home,
And its berries make a jelly which is eaten with shot game,
In Nordic lands its wood was used for making runes and sturdy walking sticks,
And crosses made from Rowan causes the devil to transfix.

The Yew a sacred tree of Celtic tribes, who lived in our fair land,

But Longbows made from English Yew, gave archers the whip hand,

At Agincourt and Crécy they felled the mounted knights,

And our victorious armies put the enemy to flight.

The Elm a tall and stately tree graces our countryside,

Though ravaged by a deadly foe that caused many trees to die,

 It's used to made divining rods, and coffins where the dead are laid

It does not rot in water so ships keels from it are made.

If you wander by a stream the Osier lines its banks,

This Willows used for baskets, cricket bats and chair back blanks,

Its weeping branches form a bower woven in natures loom,

And Willow binds the besom of a flying witch's broom.

The autumn gaudy Maples with their leaves of reds and browns,

Bedecks our varied countryside and skirts the edge of towns,

In spring it gives us syrup which on pancakes can be spread,

Whilst smoking food with maple chips makes a treat when put on bread.

The Hawthorn is a regal tree from which Maypoles were often made,

And children danced around them in many a woodland glade,

It's used for protection when formed into a hedge,

And people sealed their love with a sacred hawthorn pledge.

The Birch with bark of silver, sweeps the old year out,

And burns brightly as the yule log of that there is no doubt,

The bark was used for many things such as the making of canoes,

And cradles made from Birch wood evil spirits did bemuse.

The Holly and the Ivy herald the start of Christmas time,

They provide the greenery as joyful bells do chime,

It's said to give protection and lightning strikes are quelled

But bad luck follows people if Holly trees are felled.

The Beech tree is a symbol of the written word,

And chairs made from Beech is a craft that's still preserved,

It can be clipped to form a hedge that's dense and shaped in form

Whilst large estates plant Beeches to add stature to their lawn.

All these trees they tell us tales that folk lore does surround,

A magical journey in which legend does abound,

Man and nature are entwined, in all the tales they tell,

And please walk carefully in woods it's where the fairies dwell.

The old pack bridge at Ringley near Bolton Lancashire spans the River Irwell. A wooden bridge was first built on the site but it was washed away in a flood in 1673 and the present grade 2 listed Pack Bridge was constructed in 1677 at a cost of £500. This poem links the events, trades and people of the area, with the bridge

# RINGLEY BRIDGE SPANNING THE AGES

Men built the bridge to last for years,
People stood on it midst laughter and tears,
Spanning the ages it stood firm and solid,
This landmark spanned a river polluted and squalid.

The view from this place overlooking the vale,
With coal mines and mills all part of this tale,
People worked hard midst grime and with cotton,
For meagre wages, now gone and forgotten.

Handlooms they clattered in houses about,
For if they don't work the weavers get 'nowt,
This upstart from Bolton a man known as Crompton,
Has sounded a warning to weavers.

The miner he pauses on his way home from pit,
And looks down the road that the gas lamps had lit,
He thinks of his life spent deep in the earth,
Midst roof falls and danger and how little coal's worth.

The young man he ponders the scene over all,
He's joined Kitchener's army and answered the call,
Fate has decreed he'll be one of the fallen,
His name on a plaque oft seen, but forgotten.

A land fit for heros the banners do say,
When the guns were silenced on Armistice Day,
The bridge is still here, but jobs there are none,
And marchers from Jarrow tramp on and on.

The thirties were gay but life still was hard,
For all honest people in't paper mill yard,
But a man in Berlin not part of this scene,
Moved soldier's o'er Europe a malevolent scheme.

The Dark Age is with us and Britain's at war;
The bombers fly over all know what's in store,
Six years did pass before lights shone again;
To light up the bridge and the church down the lane,

Years since the war have seen many changes,
Yet the bridge has been rebuilt for future ages
Lovers now stand and look down o're the scene,
They now see a river that clear sweet and clean.

# GARDEN SCENE

I look around my garden and the joy it gives me shows,
The Delphiniums and Saliva in neat and ordered rows,
The lawn a dark green carpet, it shimmers in the sun
That plays upon the Hollyhocks where ants and beetles run,
The birdbath in the center is well used from dawn till dusk,
Rose's petals fall so gently and are trampled in the dust,
Geraniums like sentries stand upright and so straight,
Whilst the Clematis winds its tentacles around the garden gate
Sparrows and blue tits on the feeder swing
And the garden chime rings softly as though on angel's wings
How can there be a place that is mellower and serene
Than the vision and the beauty of my summer garden scene.

This poem is the result of my granddaughter Bex, being told by her Granddad that the sheep in the steep valleys of Lancashire were bred with two legs shorter on one side so that they would not fall over! This was because all the sheep, when I told her this piece of nonsense where facing the same way.

# NORTHERN SHEEP

Do you know that in Lanky and Yorkshire,

A special kind of sheep has been bred,

They have inside legs two inches shorter than t'other,

So on't hills they don't go heels over head.

The farmers have bred 'em that way,

As they got fed up with 'em standing askew,

For the slope of the ground made it hard for to stand,

Up straight and o'nt level like woolly sheep al'us should do,

Lanky sheep were all bred left handed

Inside leg shorter than right,

Which meant on' t hill they did point to the west,

With their bums to the east during night.

Now Yorkies were ace about face see,

With rears to the west as was right,

With all rumps pointing Lanky so no Hanky Panky,

When it comes to which slope was right.

So now as you ride down the Valley,

With all sheep faced proper way,

With face east or west depending what's best

You now know why they all stand that way.

I love fishing and have spent many happy hours looking at scenes like this.

# BESIDE A STREAM

Sitting at the side of woodland stream
The graceful willows frame the scene,
And rushes stem the waters flow,
Hiding nests that do not show,
Shy coots and moorhens with their brood,
Provide a magic interlude,
A flash of colour from a branch,
As a kingfisher performs an aquatic dance,
And emerging from the flowing stream
Providing her brood with fish cuisine,
And stately swans, cygnets in tow,
Cruise under branches hanging low,
Whilst fish rise up to feast on nymphs,
So small that we can only glimpse;
A water vole scurries by;
But I can barely catch his eye,
The rustling wind stirs the trees,
As they all dance in the breeze,
A perfect way to spend an hour,
In nature's precious woodland bower.

# STONE WALLS

They stretch for miles those walls of stone in Britain's countryside.

Made by men long ago, as they farmed the land both far and wide.

The stones they cleared, so they could plough or keep their beasts together.

And walls they built from stones dug up, that could withstand the weather.

The stones were placed so carefully, no mortar used to bind.

So the dry stone craft slowly evolved, with land enclosed, aligned.

This country's northern landscape, of limestone, millstone grit.

With miles of walled enclosures, made up of stones that fit.

For mile on mile they stand there, uphill down deepest dale.

A wind break from the tortured wind that sometimes it assails.

And in between those ancient stones, live field mouse, bird and shew.

Sheltering from the elements, just like human people do.

When you gaze at these living walls with lichen growing free.

It is the heritage of our countryside preserved for you and me.

Though built by hardy artisans, in ages long since passed.

Men still toil to mend the walls, so the art and craft will last.

# POPPIES

They grow amid the flowers so wild,

Their dancing heads by the wind beguiled,

Peeping out of tangled mass

They climb above the swaying grass,

Scarlet flashes from afar you see,

The sun on heads so wild and free,

Bees criss cross the swaying flowers

Making honey in hidden bowers,

Red poppy heads with centres black,

Sway beside the dusty track,

A nation's symbol for men of valour,

Sadly millions gone to war's Valhalla.

# MOONLIGHT

We know when we walk in the moonlight, that the shadows seem dark and surreal,

And our hearing's enhanced as we listen, for sounds that are strange and ethereal,

For when walking alone in the night-time, fear sometimes causes unease,

And shadows distort our perception, which causes our body to freeze,

An owl swoops silently past me, on patrol for a night-time snack,

And its shadow flashing by in the moonlight, makes me stop as I'm taken aback,

The church with its steeple in shadow, and a graveyard so silent and still,

Makes me think of the people who lie there, the thought of it makes me feel ill,

Writers write books about demons, with vampires well to the fore,

But a heart beating fast in the half light, is a feeling that's hard to ignore,

The light plays such tricks with your vision, and your mind misinterprets what's there

And a cold sweat breaks out in the darkness, and you just stand there and stare,

When movement returns to your body, you rush to get home safe and sound

But remember when walking in moonlight, you never know what is around.

# MY PROBLEM LOO

So happy to announce that my problem loo is sorted,
For I was so embarrassed that the flush was so
distorted,
It sounded like a fog horn from a massive ocean liner
Whenever someone used the loo it hammered like a
miner,
I tried in desperation to remedy the noise that
emanated,
That I was not successful was so ably demonstrated,
So I had to get a plumber to fettle up my loo,
He did so in a trice, so I can have a silent poo!!

# FLY AWAY

I bought myself a squirting spray,
To kill the fly that haunts my day,
The man who sold it said to me,
It would blast the fly to infinity,
I stalked the house from dawn to dusk,
But could only find neat piles of dust,
The fly alas could not be found,
And so I wander all around,
No time to read or watch TV,
That fly will be the death of me,
I walk around a soul possessed,
I cannot sleep, I cannot rest,
Until I see that fly is dead
And I can safely go to bed.

# SCHOOL HOLIDAYS

The holidays have started, six weeks away from school.
The kids are all excited, play is the golden rule.
Now mum and dad have six weeks, to entertain their brood.
To go on walks and cycle rides, with picnic finger food.
But soon the dreaded words were heard, " Oh Mum I do feel bored."
It's said amidst a room that's where, their toys and games are stored.
Piled high amidst computers, electronic games and such.
A lonely little figure says, "I do not like them much,"
It seems imagination has departed from his brain.
As he cannot think of anything, his excuse to mum is lame.
In total exasperation, mum tries to make things right.
But still the moody little tyke won't go and fly his kite.
He wants to go on holiday, to far flung foreign lands.
Just like Johnny down the street, who'll come back nice and tanned.
Money's tight for families, it just does not grow on trees.
And kids have got to understand, their whines mums can't appease.
Soon they will be back at school, and sanity returns.
To lots of harassed Mums and Dads, from their six week school sojourn.

# PARENTAL JOY!!

The house is nice and quiet, the kids are back at school.

My hearing now is normal, my voice sounds kind of cool.

I cannot hear the bleatings of siblings falling out.

And toys cascading down the stairs and Lego strewn about.

My mind is now so peaceful Nirvana I have reached.

My partner's here beside me the noisy ship has beached.

Just for a few hours peace reigns in our silent home.

Before the children reappear and the quiet time is blown.

A neighbour knowing that I was a retired nurse was telling me about her "woman's problem" and I could not resist writing a poem about it. This amused her a lot but she then said that I had to write a verse about a problem men had. The next two poems highlight their problems .

# MI PROBLEM

I have a "woman's problem" O please, Oh please don't tell,
I've had it for a little while, but now it gives me hell,
My "thingy's," out of order, my bits are falling out,
I'll have to get it sorted, of that there is no doubt,
I've heard that they could fit a ring, but how does that help me,
My fingers do not cause me pain; it's the bottom end you see,
My "playpen gear" has lost its bounce, my undercarriage broke,
I don't fancy any doctor giving my "thingy" a prod and poke.
So I just sit and wonder how soon the doctor calls
To mend a broken "thingy", before the blooming lot just falls.

# NO MORE KIDS!

M i wife has put her foot down; she's stated no more
kids,

She says that she can't take the pill; an I've to do as she
bids,

I'm feared to ask mi mates as to what they have had
done,

And it makes me so embarrassed, to have a stop light on
mi fun,

The sultans in their harems had men's dangly bits
removed,

The removal of their urge to merge left what remained
quite bruised,

I think that is rather drastic to contemplate such action,

And cutting off mi pride and joy does not have much
attraction,

It seems that you can have an op, that needs a little cut,

And a local anesthetic means, you don't feel it much,

I had it done at clinic, and it was over in a trice

Mi firing pin the doc removed, and he was so precise,

When I walked out of clinic, I was bow legged and in
pain,

With a walk that resembled that great cowboy Mr.
Wayne,

So now I have my pleasure, and no kids can now ensue

But unfortunately it left me, with a walk that's still askew!

# THE FRIENDLY NEIGHBOUR

I have a friendly neighbour, she nearly drives me wild,

I see her peeping through her nets, she's like a little child,

Her eyes they miss nothing, and her hearing is acute.

Without a doubt she must be; the districts biggest "toot",

News of any "Hanky Panky" that happens hereabout.

Finds its way to her door, of that there is no doubt,

Her network of informants must rival MI5,

Her information super highway just makes her gossip thrive,

No need for a computer, it's all filed in her head.

And she can tell you if your relatives, are alive or dead,

Your husband can not go out, without her knowing where,

And if there any chance of dalliance, I'll bet that she'll be there!

I'll swear she has the marriage lines, of every one in't street.

And any living "overt brush", she would not be discreet.

If anyone is pregnant, she knows as soon as they.

And if they're married or engaged, or merely "played away."

So you can see in out street, you have to be as white as driven snow.

Or our friendly neighbour down the street, will soon be in the know.

42

I have always been a cat person and this poem for me sums up all the aristocratic aloofness of certain cats.

# CROMPTON CAT

I walk with head and tail erect, a regal bearing as you would expect,
From such a cat as you can see, nobility exudes from me,
And as I walk most cats would bow, she cats curtsy or kowtow,
For they can see I am aloof, from common cat's as I'm the proof,
That good manners and selective breeding, and being adept at public speaking
All combine to raise my tone, a high born cat who walks alone,
The name of Crompton says it all, for I was born in stately hall,
Away from all the hoi-polloi, who don't know breeding not at all,
Some say that I'm a snob, they are just jibes from the common mob,
The Lady Jane, my owner, says "I am the best", as on silk cushions I do rest,
Though Croft the butler does not like, to hear me, when I roam at night,
Whilst I do rounds to make quite sure, that mice don't roam or breed galore,
You see I have a tranquil life; with very little toil and strife,
I live with elite upper classes, and can't abide the common masses!

My dear wife Pat battled cancer for 12 years until her death in 2013.She contracted breast cancer in 2000 and had 2 years treatment and was then pronounced clear.

However it returned in her bones 2011

I was her carer until she passed away in a hospice in 2013. These poems were written both during the time I cared for her, and also after her death. I have found that for me it was helpful in the grieving process to write down what I felt. This was better than keeping it locked up inside me. She was the most Loyal, Honest, and Courageous person I have ever met and I love and miss her so much.

# A CARER'S VIEW

It's 3 o'clock in the morning and the light is on in your room,

Just as hundreds of others like you, you look out and gaze at the moon,

But you are not there just to moon gaze, whilst there is a job to be done,

You look at the person you care for, and continue to help your loved one,

You get no days off for your pleasure, no overtime or holidays with pay,

You do it because they need you, both during the night and the day,

The commitment you give must be total, your love unbounded and true,

But it's hard at times to be cheerful, with always an optimist's view,

At times you get very discouraged, when things just don't go to plan,

It's nobody's fault you're just tired, not made like a storybook superman,

We do save the country a fortune, but we do it for love not kudos.

We care and we nurse and we cherish, so loved ones will never feel lost,

 Now as I write this short poem, it says all that has to be said,

For I've nursed, cooked, cleaned and have polished, now I stagger off to my bed.

# THE CARER

I'm just a husband, who gives care to my wife,

When cancer struck 2 years ago it completely changed our life,

We were at first bewildered and angry and so sad,

And if the truth be known as well, it also made us mad,

We had such a pleasant life with trips and holidays,

But now the curse of cancer tries to dominate our days

All the trips to doctors the X rays and the tests,

When all my dear wife wants to do is sit at home and rest,

Our roles have been switched over; I now cook the tea and wash,

And make the bed, iron the clothes and try to make things posh,

I do get lots of "guidance" from my supervising wife,

I know that I'm not as good as her, at this "multitasking" life,

For good or bad I married her, and this bit can be bad,

But I love her and she knows it, so that does not make me sad,

We cannot change the cards we're dealt along the path of life,

And looking after her just shows that I cherish my dear wife.

# LOSS

My darling wife is no more, her presence gone,
She leaves a space within my air which will never fill,
I hear her voice in silent moments, as I recall the times we shared,
Her laughter follows me like rippling waves on the sea shore,
I gaze at flowers, but only see the ones that gave her joy,
The stately Iris, upright and strong with regal beauty,
Carnations long lasting and steadfast as her love,
The Magnolia bursts forth as she welcomed people with a smile,
I sit in silence and alone, wrapped in a blanket of memories and love.
Yet she would not wish me to descend to misery and despair,
Her love of life will gently guide me on the path to bright tomorrows,
Like the pain she bravely bore, my pain will ease in time,
And what will remain is a treasured place for her within my soul.

# GRIEF

She may be gone but deep within my being there lives a memory.

I look up at the stars and imagine that each one is a departed soul.

It's comforting to know that, looking to the stars provides a focus.

Our loved ones are represented there in endless time and space.

The body that we saw that breathed no more is just an empty shell.

Devoid of life, but the soul has travelled far into the cosmos

Perhaps to be reborn into another being, continuing the wheel of life.

There remains our memories of shared laughter, and silent tears.

Of places cherished, and friends visited, we feel the loss,

It is for ourselves we grieve, but memories never die.

# THOUGHTS

My dear wife Pat though she has gone,
Her presence in my home lives on,
For every day, no matter what I do,
I feel her presence as photos I look through,
The memories come flooding back,
Of times we spent walking down a track,
Or sitting fishing by some lake,
Anxiously waiting for the fish to take,
And when at home we'd sit and say,
That we had had a perfect day,
No need to talk whilst sitting there,
Just being together made us aware,
That silence you can share with ease,
Just sitting listening, to the breeze,
The gap within my life's still there,
So many things I long to share,
A book, a poem, to feel her there,
But that's a dream that can never be,

All I have are thoughts of thee.

# HOSPICE

When I could no longer cope with her care I'm glad the hospice it was there,

Though it broke my heart to see her leave, the months of pressure it did relive

I knew then that she would not return, so my emotions began to churn,

Was it right that she should go, into a place we both did not know?

I saw that look upon her face, as we went into the hospice gate,

But uncomplaining she did what's best, so I could get some peace and rest,

At what cost I asked myself, did I her decision compel,

They greeted her with care, compassion and kindness filled the air,

I loved her then with all my heart, but knew that soon our ways must part,

Just sitting there and holding hands we talked of holidays in far off lands,

Some staff we knew from times long gone, but now we had to soldier on,

My dear one ill but not in pain, we sat and watched the falling rain.

Through the window we both did see, the birds and squirrels in the trees,

A tranquil, silent, place of care, we had no thoughts of leaving there,

But slowly as the days went by, we both knew soon that she would die,

Sat by her bed I watched her go, I felt just numb and very low,

Its 6 months since that time of grief, I still miss her with no relief,

In time I'm sure the pain will ease, people try to help, appease,

I'm not sure if I did what's best, or was it just to get some rest?

That answer I will never know, but my love for her will grow and grow.

# WE GO TO CHURCH

Some go to church to say a prayer, some go to
church because it there,
Some go to just be seen to go, whilst others go when
they feel low,
Some go to just look around, and some to hear the
organ's sound,
Some go because the vicar's nice, and some to be as
quiet as mice,
Some go because they love to sing, and some to hear
the church bells ring,
Some go because their conscience pricks, and some
to hear the holy scripts
Some go to name a baby small, and feel
embarrassed when they bawl!
Some to hear the marriage banns, then in marriage
join their hands.
Some go when they depart this life and leave a
grieving husband, wife.
Why people go to the church's call, is personal to
one and all,
There is to all who venture there, a quiet peaceful
special air
And in our own way we do pray, to guide our feet
upon life's way,
Let us hope that we can be, a credit to God's family,
Show kindness, comfort, and charity, to those whose
lives may need all three.

# CHRISTMAS MORN

It's Christmas morn but still abed,

Are lots of sleepy little heads,

Last night they waited full of joy,

For presents for each girl and boy,

But soon they will all awake,

And joyous sounds each child shall make,

The magic of this Christmas morn,

When years ago the Christ child was born.

The joy and love that now abounds,

Fills each home with precious sounds.

# THOUGHTS FOR CHRISTMAS

I've just got round to thinking what Christmas is about,
It's not about the parties and rushing in and out,
It's not about the presents and the drinking till you drop,
Nor Christmas cards, or Christmas trees with fairies on the top,
It has a deeper meaning that really should come first,
It's all about a tiny child who had a virgin birth,
It's all about a person who came to show the way
That we could just change our lives, if we would stop and say,
What can I do for other folk? Who find that life is sad,
How can I make a difference? to change to good, the bad.
Let's think about the old and young, spending Christmas all
alone,
Invite them in to share with you, the joy of what you own,
It does not have to be too grand, just simple homely fare,
Just as that old innkeeper keeper gave a stable that was bare,
Think on these things at Christmas time and throughout the
year,
You will find, it really is, a season of good cheer.

# THE SCOTS NEW YEAR

The Christmas splurge is over,
Waistlines no longer trim,
All presents have been opened,
To see what lay within,
The highland folk get ready;
To drink from dusk till dawn,
With not a care it seems to me;
Their accounts are overdrawn,
The whisky it just flows and flows,
As on "first footing" they embark,
To all their drunken neighbours,
Who find it such a lark
A bottle in the one hand,
And a haggis in the other,
And wearing tartan underpants,
From the cold that makes them shudder,
"Good luck" to all you Sassenachs,
You hear the Scots men cry,
To inebriated English men who chance to pass them by.
So look forward to the New Year,
In your alcoholic haze,
With prices up and rising VAT, in nearing future days.

# ELF AND SAFETY CHRISTMAS

Our Town Halls cancelled Christmas or so I have been
told,
It's because of Elf and Safety for they want total control,
They have looked at all the trimmings that Christmas always
brings,
And have written regulations to mess up yuletide things,
Our man first looked at Christmas trees, they were, he said
"too tall,"
The wind might blow them down you see, if there was a nasty
squall,
No more than one foot high he said in case the wind blew
strong
And coloured lights and baubles, would be he said "just
wrong"
Mistletoe you must not hang, for kissing it is banned
As winter flu is all about, in this infected land!
Next he looked at Santa's sleigh, the air brakes were not right
And a regulation flight plan, must be submitted Christmas
night
For Air traffic controllers must have their little say
They are worried about low flying, in built up areas Christmas
day!
It cannot Snow at Christmas, for the gritters will not work
Its triple time for them you see, or their duties they will shirk
The safety man's got a problem, regarding flying poo
For Rudolph and his cohorts, won't stop and use a loo
Our man is very worried, about things falling from on high,
And crashing on the heads, of inebriated passersby,
He will be out with his little meter, saying "those carols
are too loud "
To protect all people's eardrums, is an aim he has avowed.
So let it be a silent night; no sleigh bells to be heard,
To satisfy the safety man the jumped up little nerd!

56

# BOOKS

It lies there on the table just waiting to be read,
Beneath its hard back covers bound with linen
thread,
The authors weaves their magic, with special tales to
tell,
And you the reader cannot wait to fall beneath their
spell,
Some books they draw you right away, into their
special world
Whilst others tantalize and twist, their secrets to
unfurl,
It does not matter where you are, in wood or busy
train,
The world inside their pages is your mystical
domain,
You settle down to read a book, your whole
demeanor changes
The outside world it disappears, whilst you delve
into its pages,
You are lost within its special world, its characters
are real,
Displaying all emotions, that we human people feel,
The authors can transport us, to far and distant
lands,
Or have us wander aimlessly beside a coastal strand,
I could not live without my books, they are to me a
treasure
They fill my life with happiness and brighten up my
leisure.

# FLAT PACK

My friend bought a flat pack from Ikea down the road.

The salesman said that home delivery, would ease a heavy load.

To make it would be easy, a child could assemble it.

With a handbook full of diagrams, to make sure that all parts fit.

She bought a desk and wardrobe, to fit in her new room.

Where wi fi , printer and computer, would light the evenings gloom.

Cardboard filled the room, as the flat pack was unfurled.

The bits all packed so neatly in this high tech packaged world.

Screws and fastening all displayed, in sizes small to large.

Printed in the instruction book, so you can just take charge.

At first it seemed so simple, but then confusion did appear.

And sorting all the various bits, did not seem so clear.

Crawling on the floor made the knees a little sore.

Whilst assembling all the various bits seemed, more than a little chore.

Slowly the desk it did appear, but assembly caused contortions.

To get the parts in order, in the proper right proportions.

One's head got jammed inside the drawers, to turn the screws was tricky.

Whilst observers to this twisted freak, began to take the micky.

At last the job was finished, and the desk was finally done.

Despite all the varied problems, the battle it was won.

After resisting buying a computer for a considerable length of time, I was persuaded to purchase one by my wife. I was terrified of messing the thing up, and also did not understand the alien language that people who knew about computers spoke. This poem speaks of my terror at the time.

(If I mess my computer up now, I just ask my daughter-in-law to sort it out for me !)

# SILVER SURFER

I now have reached the golden age and work no longer beckons

Naught to do but sit around, or read a book I reckons,

But this idyllic lifestyle was soon to be disjointed,

When to the world of computers,   friends moving fingers pointed,

My poor heart started pounding and sweat was on my brow,

I'll get a book and study, about computers just for now,

But the book was full Gigabytes, and thumbnails and of RAMs

But I did not know that computers, has 'owt to do with lambs,

I did not understand a word, of all the things I read,

To me it seems senility, had rendered my brain dead.

With heavy heart, and very twitched, I shelled out lots of loot

Only to be told at once, my laptop needs a boot!

I wondered did it need a sock? Because the case was tight,

But kicking it into the road, did not seem quite right.

Just flick the switch and turn it on, there's nothing left to fear

I just hope that when I do, a computer geek is near,

It's a machine just like a car and all should be ok,

And if the screen starts flashing, it would really make my day,

Across the screen it says windows, but I see only one,

What happened to all the others they seem to have all gone?

I'm told it has a mother board but why has she gone down?

I have not done anything to make her scowl and frown,

A man he mentioned E-Mails but what the heck are they?

He says they are just like letters, but postage you don't pay,

You have to have some software, I think that wool is soft,

But a woolly clad computer, what happens when it's washed?

With all these many questions, whizzing round in my poor head,

I just can't take it in; I think my brain is dead.

They say go surf the internet but a beach I do not see,

And I have not got a surf board that just belongs to me.

Basic is a language, that's used by techno geeks,

But to me it's complicated, I don't understand when he speaks,

So you can see the level, of my techno geeky savvy,

Computers are just not for me, I'll go and make some coffee!

I do have a smart phone, when a friend asked what was my number ,I could not find it on my phone , this poem is the result !!

# SMART PHONE

I've got myself a smart phone because I think I'm smart,
But how to switch the darn thing on, was not a glorious start,
The salesman said I needed it, so I would be up to date and trendy
I bought it because he was so nice, I should not be unfriendly,
He said that it had lots of Aps, but what the heck are those?
I know that Alps are mountains, but I'll learn I do suppose,
He said that it was for four Gee Gee, but a horse I do not want,
And riding on a saddle appears not my safest jaunt,
He said that I can text the world, and gave me the hardest sell,
But the letters are oh so small, and I cannot see too well,
You can also search the internet and do a Google search,
But not knowing what a Google is, has left me in the lurch,
A built in sort of Sat. Nav. means, that I know where I am at,
But a wandering mind is a problem that resides beneath my hat,
It has a digital camera, to take pictures as I stroll,
But how to get the pictures out, must surely take its toll,
This techno geeky marvel, has got me so confused,
My head feels sort of twisted, and my mind it feels so bruised
It seems that I am not the man, to make a new fresh start
I think I'll have to ditch the phone, it appears I'm not so smart!

# MY PEEPERS

I had to go to the hospital to have my peepers checked.

It seemed to the optician that my eyesight it was wrecked.

They sent me a letter which said what time to go.

So early in the morning too, when my brain was going slow.

They told me not to drive there, as my eyes had to have some drops.

My eyesight it went crazy, kind of fuzzy and in knots.

They sat me at a weird machine, a light shining in my eye.

Whilst my chin was held quite tightly, and I did not feel so spry.

The nurse said she'd take some images, to show up any strictures.

But all I saw was flashing lights; I could not see no pictures!

Half blinded I wandered round, no white stick did I see.

All I wanted was a tin cup, and a beggar I would be.

At last I saw a doctor, who said one eye was shot.

But the other one made up for it, which cheered me up a lot.

All this to get new glasses, it seemed a right to do.

Now I'm back to the optician, and bid the hospital Adieu!

# THE GOLDEN YEARS

They say that it's the golden age, when you reach sixty plus,
But now that I have reached it, my gold has turned to dust,
My once trim waist has now enlarged, and what was once petite
Now spreads in larger circles, towards my puffed up swollen feet,
They say that you must exercise, and walk and run and ski,
But how the heck can this be, when arthritis ails each knee,
My spine no longer supple, my back is like a board,
My joints they go on creaking like a clapped out battered Ford,
My water works now make me rise from out of bed each night
And I can't find the light switch as my eyesight's not quite right!
My hair it's started falling out and gets thinner every day,
It once was my crowning glory, now its just sort of grey,
My brain though it's still working, but the odd thing slips my mind,
I'm having senior moments; it's my glasses I can't find!
These Golden years are special or so the experts say,
For you to just enjoy life and relish every day,
That's fine if all your body parts, work like an oiled machine,
Life's rusted up my body, with its vintage aging sheen,
O golden years why do you do, these horrid thing to me?
I always thought that in these years, I would be fancy free,
I'd go and explore the Spanish Main, or find some buried treasure,
Instead I take my medicines, and watch "tele" at my leisure!

# PAIN

Some folks call them just a pain, but I find them ok
It does not mean that they are ill, in a medical kind of way,
Pains do in fact all vary, in lots of different ways,
Some complain of shooting pains, they get on rainy days,
Whilst arthritis causes aches, in fingers and in joints,
And scalds and blisters, they appear, when with hot water we anoint,
A throbbing head is not too nice, when migraine takes a bow,
But lumbago has me in its grip and I cannot move just now,
A trip to the dentist looms, when toothache drives you wild,
And "growing pains" afflicted you, when you were just a child
Shooting, aching, throbbing in scales of one to ten,
Though I am told they differ in women and in men,
Men I'm told are very soft, when it comes to bearing pain,
But women are much braver so the females always claim,
So as you see the next time, you feel the slightest twinge,
Fill yourself with aspirin and for heaven's sake don't whinge!

# SLEEP

You toss and turn and try to sleep,
Close your eyes and count the sheep,
But that's a laugh, it does not work,
Your mind it just goes berserk,
For the sheep they roam and can't be found,
And with eyes wide open you look around,
All you see is darkened room;
Dressing table with perfume,
The doctor said he'd give you pills,
To cure your nocturnal sleepless ills,
But still you toss and turn in bed,
They just give you a "woolly" head,
Maybe my evening nap,
In front of "TV" I should scrap,
Then I'm sure I would feel "beat",
And at night, I'd get a decent sleep!!

# HORACE FLYNN

Horace Flynn was very thin, a matchstick did seem fatter,
His appetite was very good, but his waistline did not flatter,
His doctor did advise him, to go to sunnier climes,
So off he went to the airport, to check on flying times.
He rather fancied Texas, as cowboys he did like,
And he fancied roping steers, after riding through the night.
He'd like to do a round up, and branding cows looked fun.
But all this riding horses, might play havoc with his bum.
A dude ranch seemed the answer, to his quest to adding
pounds,
He thought that lots of steaks and beans, would make his
body round.
He arrived in sunny Texas, and to the shops did go.
To get appropriate dress for his dude cowboy show.
His hat was half a gallon, for ten gallon would not fit.
His jeans they had a slackness, which showed a generous fit.
When asked what 'chaps' he would like he replied
"I'm not like that!"
And boots and spurs were miniscule, just like his tiny hat.
The getup looked ridiculous, but he thought that he looked
grand.
But when he tried to mount a horse, he needed a helping
hand.
Off to the ranch he did ride, his bum and saddle oft did
collide.
The bunk house first caught his eye, it looked a mess
and was not spry.
The bunks small and rather snug, and a cowboy's life seemed
none too good.
He laid upon his lumpy bed, false dreams whirling in his
head.

At daybreak on the following day, he went to feed a cow some hay.

The cow it took a mighty bite, and Horace got dredful fright. It missed his fingers by a whisker, so shocked he downed a tot of liquor,

And shaking still and somewhat hazy, he thought this cow poke business crazy.

Still off he went to get his chow, baked beans and a steak of cow.

This diet really gave him hell, his rear end produced a sound and smell.

The sound went with him as he walked, and interrupted when he talked.

But still here t'was common place, the cow pokes suffered no disgrace.

They showed him how to rope a steer, all Horace did was shake with fear.

The steer it wildly ran about, "please go slow" Horace did shout.

He tried in vain to catch the beast, all he lassoed was a passing priest.

Branding was the next big test, so Horace stripped down to his vest.

Branding iron was placed in hand, and over steers rump he did stand.

But true to form the brand did slip, and Horace got Bar X on hip.

This caused him to scream and holler, I'm off home by noon tomorra.

He packed and flew home the next day, not one day more would he stay.

So now he walks with Bar X on hip, a stark reminder of his trip.

There is a clock on my wall that my father bought in about 1916, for my Mum just after they were married. It saw the passage of all the ups and downs of our typical family.

# MY MUMS CLOCK

The clock it hangs upon the wall it was bought in nineteen sixteen,
Dad bought it for my mum, and on her wall it's always been
It marked the time when the Kaiser roared and my dad he went to war.
He came back a troubled man with memories of its gore,
Whilst ticking on, it saw the birth, of babies numbered six
Two died in childhood leaving, two boys, two girls, the mix,
It ticked on through the Second World War, not harmed by Manchester's blitz.
Flames rose high in the red streaked sky, from bombs, dropped by Fritz,
Our clock it marked the time, when wars Victory did arrive
But when dad died it stopped for him, as though it was alive,
It started after a short time, then charted days of bliss,
As wedding bells rang, for members of our family, sealed with a loving kiss,
Sadly a daughter's tragedy meant changes to mums life,
She became her children's guardian, to save them from more strife,
The clock it kept on ticking through the stages of their life
And watched each girl flee the nest, each to became a wife,
Mum and her clock had aged a lot, and when the Good Lord called,
It bade farewell, and stopped again, with the mechanism stalled.
It still ticks on though times have changed but now it does reside,
On her son's wall ticking still, charting times relentless tide.

# WAR

We see each week a war on film
In Europe and in far flung lands,
With patriotic trumpet blasts
And soldiers marching guns in hands,
Why do we always think it's right?
To crush opponents with superior might
When it's been proved time and again
That talk is the solution to civilian pain
The greed that lies within men's souls,
To have more land or just control,
Seems to override the peoples will
To live in peace and not just kill,
Someday I hope that peace will thrive,
And to that end we all must strive,
Maybe my dream I will not see
A world at peace to eternity.

**Also available from Violet Circle Publishing.**

**Heirs to the Kingdom By Robin John Morgan**.

Seek out another wonderful and captivating slice of life Adventure Fantasy with Robin John Morgan's Heirs to the Kingdom.

Take a walk in the woodland where you will find a whole new kind of world, as it recovers from the Red Death, a virus that has wiped out the modern world as we know it today.

Set in the year 2038 Heirs to the Kingdom is a tale of life set inside the struggle of the town of Loxley, as a prophecy made in the year AD 421 predicts the rising of a bowman who will seek out the new heirs to the kingdom of Britain.

Join the fight as the evil Mason Knox tries to take the land for his own, only to face a young boy with an unnatural talent with a long bow. This is a tale of a captivating adventure with laughter, tears and magic from a time long since passed, superbly crafted by Author Robin John Morgan.

Take a walk in the woodland today:

Heirs to the Kingdom Book One : The Bowman of Loxley
ISBN 978-1-910299-00-5 Violet Circle Publishing.

Heirs to the Kingdom Book Two : The Lost sword of Carnac
ISBN 978-1-910299-01-2 Violet Circle Publishing.

Heirs to the Kingdom Book Three : The Darkness of Dunnottar
ISBN 978-1-910299-02-9 Violet Circle Publishing

Heirs to the Kingdom Book Four : Queen of the Violet Isle
ISBN 978-1-910299-03-6 Violet Circle Publishing.

Keep up to date with some wonderful books at
www.violetcirclepublishing.co.uk.

Violet Circle Publishing. Manchester. UK.

www.violetcirclepublishing.co.uk